MARY,
MOTHER OF RECONCILIATIONS

MARY

MOTHER OF
RECONCILIATIONS

Mother Teresa of Calcutta
Brother Roger of Taizé

PAULIST PRESS
New York/Mahwah

Selection and arrangement of texts © Les Presses de Taize
1987. First published 1987 by A.R. Mowbray & Co. Ltd,
Saint Thomas House, Becket Street, Oxford OX1 1SJ.
Published in The United States of America in 1989 by
Paulist Press, 997 Macarthur Boulevard, Mahwah, New
Jersey 07430.

Library of Congress Cataloging-in-Publication Data

Teresa, Mother, 1910-
    Mary, Mother of Reconciliation/ by Mother Teresa
of Calcutta & Brother Roger of Taize.
        p.   cm.
    ISBN 0-8091-3063-7 $3.95
    1. Mary, Blessed Virgin, Saint. I. Roger, frere,
1915-   II. Title.
BT602.T46   1989
232.91—dc19

                                              89-2854
                                              CIP

Printed and bound in the
United States of America

CONTENTS

MARY, MOTHER OF RECONCILIATIONS

Saint John, in his great age, could only keep repeating: God is love. Where God is, there is love.

We, all of us, can bring the love of Jesus to others and become a ferment of reconciliation, not only among believers but in the entire human family.

May our homes, however modest they may be, become like the house of Mary in Nazareth: a place to welcome people to prayer, a place of reconciliation.

And Mary will be for us 'mother of reconciliations'.

MOTHER TERESA AND BROTHER ROGER

1

HANDMAID OF THE LORD

Mother Teresa

Gentle and humble of heart

The greatness of the Virgin Mary, like our own greatness, lies in humility. That is absolutely necessary for us. Even if people love us and appreciate our work, we must always remain humble, for our work is not ours but God's work.

Let the example of Our Lady make our hearts meek and humble like that of her Son. In her the heart of Jesus was formed. Let us learn to be humble, accepting humility with joy. We have been created for great things; why should we lower ourselves to things that would soil the beauty of our hearts? It is so easy to be proud, heartless, selfish—yes, so easy; but we have been created for much greater things.

How much we can learn from Mary! She was so humble because she belonged entirely to God. She was full of grace. Ask the Virgin Mary to say to Jesus, as in Cana, 'They have no more wine. They need the wine of humility and gentleness, of goodness and kindness.' She will certainly answer us, 'Do whatever he tells you'.

Mary will teach us humility. Though full of grace yet only the handmaid of the Lord, she stands as one of us at the foot of the cross, in need of the mercy of God. Let us, like her, touch the dying, the poor, the lonely and the unwanted according to the graces we have received and let us not be ashamed or slow to do the humble work.

The tenderness of God's love

Mary can teach us kindness. 'They have no wine,' she told Jesus at Cana. Let us, like her, be aware of the needs of the poor, be they spiritual or material and let us, like her, give generously of the love and grace we are granted.

A few weeks ago two young people came to our house and they gave me lots of money to feed the people. In Calcutta, as you know, we have many, many poor people. We cook for 9,000 people every day and if we did not, they would probably not have anything to eat.

I asked these two young people, 'Where did you get so much money?' They said, 'Two days ago we got married, and before our marriage we decided that we were not going to buy wedding clothes, we were not going to have a wedding feast, we would give you the money to feed the poor.' For me it was something extraordinary to see upper-class Hindu people do that, and it was a scandal in Calcutta. And then I asked

them again, 'But why did you do that?' —
'We love each other so much that we
wanted to begin our life together by loving
others, by making a sacrifice.' They knew
what a big sacrifice that would be, and yet
they loved each other so much. They loved
others as God loves them. This is something so beautiful. This is an image of the
tenderness of God's love.

Serving others with joy

It is good for us not to be attached to one place, but to be ready and eager to cross the world. Our eagerness is the proof of a true love for God. Zeal is the test of love and the test of zeal is the ability to give our life for others. We cannot not be on fire with love for others.

We know that when Jesus came on this earth his Mother Mary took him straight away to give him to others. What did she want to do? To bring joy.

That is one of the most beautiful moments in Mary's life. As soon as Jesus entered her life she left at once, in haste, for Elizabeth's village to give Jesus to her and to the son she was expecting. We read in the Gospel that the child 'leapt for joy' in Elizabeth's womb at this first meeting with Christ.

You and I have been created for the same purpose, to bring joy and reconciliation into the world. To be able to love, to be able to love God.

Let Mary be the source of our joy. Let each one of us be Jesus for her. No one learned humility better than Mary. She was the Handmaid. Our Lady's strength lay in joy. Only joy could give her the strength to go with haste to the hill-country of Judea to do a handmaid's work, a servant's work. Being a handmaid means serving others with joy.

We too must go with haste up to the hills of difficulties, to serve others with joy.

Happy the pure in heart

Prayer always gives a clean heart, and a clean heart can see God. To see God means to love God.

Let us ask Our Lady to help us to keep our hearts pure so that we may be able to love God as God loves us and love Christ, his Son, with tenderness.

But how do we love?

The poor, the hungry, the naked, the homeless are very wonderful people and we owe them great gratitude, because they give us an opportunity to love God through them.

Some time ago, in Calcutta, we did not have sugar for our children. A little Hindu child, four years old, went home and told his parents, 'I will not eat sugar for three days; I will give my sugar to Mother Teresa'. That child loved with great love, because he loved until it hurt.

One evening, a gentleman came to our house and told me of a family with eight children that had not eaten for some days. I took some rice and went to their house. The mother took the rice and divided it into two and went out. When she came back I asked her, 'Where did you go? What did you do?' She answered, 'They are hungry too.' She knew that her neighbours were hungry. I was not surprised that she gave half of her rice.

Pray for our poor, pray for our lepers, pray for those lonely and unwanted people, the rejected, the forgotten.

Let us begin by loving our neighbours, and so fulfil God's desire that we become Carriers of his love and compassion.

Loving God's poor

Let us ask in prayer to have, like Our Lady, a tender love for God's poor people.

It is not how much we give that counts, but how much love we put in the giving. And this is what is so beautiful for young people to live.

And so I say to the young: Open your hearts to the love of God which he will give you. He loves you with tenderness. And he will give you not to keep but to share. The less you have the more you can give, and the more you have the less you can give.

When we pray, ask, ask for courage to give until it hurts. And how will we do that? By love in action.

That is what the Sisters are trying to do. It is not our vocation to serve the poorest of the poor. Our vocation is to belong to Jesus with the conviction that nothing and nobody can separate us from the love of Christ. But the work that the Church has entrusted to us is our love for Jesus in action.

What you do today as young people is your love for Jesus in action: some of you are studying, some are working, some are preparing for the future but all with that same conviction and that tremendous and tender love for Christ.

With Christ and through him we will be able to do great things. To be able to do that, we need to pray. For the fruit of prayer is the deepening of faith. And the fruit of faith is love. And the fruit of love is service.

That is why Jesus made himself the bread of life, to satisfy our hunger for him, for his love. And then, as if that was not enough for him, he made himself the hungry one, the naked one, the homeless one, so that you and I can satisfy his hunger for our human love.

And therefore let us remember what Jesus has said, 'Whatever you do to the least of my brethren, you do it to me'.

2

PRAYING WITH MARY AND THE APOSTLES

Brother Roger

A contemplative people

A good many years ago, some time before travelling to a country in Eastern Europe for a meeting with young people, I received a letter from that country:

'We are looking forward to a message from you, not just for ourselves, but for all the Christians who, throughout the world, are undergoing trials. Here is our contribution to that message:

'Our situation is comparable to that of the apostles and Mary just after the death of Christ. Jesus had suffered; he was dead; the disciples were distraught and fearful.

'But after a period of despair, like them we understood: Christ is risen! Fear and despair are already behind us; we no longer feel completely lost. Still, like the apostles, our possibilities are limited.

'We realize that, somehow, all this has happened in order that Jesus could send his Spirit. It is only a preparation for a new springtime of the Church. The important thing for us now is to recognize the specific grace that Jesus is offering us in our situation, to pray with Mary and the apostles a prayer that the Holy Spirit communicates to our hearts.

'Yes, even those who have no resources, no outward possibilities, can do this: in small communities, with their brothers and sisters, with Mary and the apostles, pray in expectant waiting for the Holy Spirit.

'That is our vocation at this time: to pray so that God's people may become a contemplative people who live lives deeply rooted in the Spirit of the Risen Christ.'

The spirit of praise

The Virgin Mary's 'yes' finds its fulfilment in an attitude of offering: in faith, simple trust in God, Mary did not hold on to her Son for herself; she gave him to the world. We too wish to find our fulfilment in trusting and, in the spirit of praise, by giving all that God gives to us.

But how can we place our trust in God when a question rises incessantly from the hearts of many: if God existed, he would not permit wars, injustice, illness and the oppression of even one human being on this earth. If God existed, he would keep us from doing evil.

In a leper hospital in Calcutta, where I was sharing the life of the poorest for a time, I saw a leper raise his arms and what remained of his hands and sing these words: 'God has not inflicted a punishment on me; I praise him because my illness has turned into a visit from God'.

On either side of him, to be sure, other lepers were moaning with pain and with despair. But this one had realized that suffering is not sent by God; it is not a consequence of wrongdoing. God is not the author of evil, nor a tormentor of the human conscience.

When certain Christian thinkers make God an enemy of life, a God who would punish in order to inspire fear and to be respected, they dig a pit for us to fall into. But the Virgin Mary has always come to fill up such an abyss. She is never depicted as someone who imposes herself by threats, who plays upon our fears. She is the one who helps us discover the Church as mother.

Listening to the leper's song in Calcutta, I seemed to be hearing Job, that believer of long ago, before Christ, on whom trials rained down. Job knew that his immense suffering was not punishment for doing wrong. And one day he discovered the spirit of praise. Like the leper of Calcutta he was able to say: 'In my trials God seeks me; I know now that my Redeemer is alive, and so my heart is burning within me'.

Why does God not prevent us from doing evil? Because he has not made human beings robots. God created us in his own image, that is, free.

When we love someone with all our heart, our love desires to leave the loved one free to respond.

God loves us with a love beyond words, and leaves us free to make a radical choice: free to love or to refuse love and to reject God; free to spread through the world a leaven of reconciliation or a ferment of injustice; free to shine with radiant communion in Christ or to tear ourselves away from it and even to destroy in others their thirst for the living God.

But God does not look on passively at the choices of human beings. God suffers along with them. Through Christ, in agony for each man and woman on this earth, by his Holy Spirit constantly active within us, God visits us even in the deserts of our hearts.

Together with Mary, turned towards the Risen Christ, we can wait in the peace of our nights, in the silence of our days, in the beauty of creation and in times of deep inner struggle—wait for our deserts to flower.

Prayer

Lord Christ, even if we had faith enough to move mountains, without love, what would we be?

You love us.

Without your Spirit who lives in our hearts, what would we be?

You love us.

By taking everything upon yourself, you open for us a way towards faith, towards trust in God, who wants neither suffering nor human distress.

Spirit of the Risen Christ, Spirit of compassion, Spirit of praise, your love for each one of us will never disappear.

A fire that never dies away

From our earliest years, there are impressions that mark us for life. When I was five, I spent one Sunday with my sisters in the region of Estavayer. Late in the afternoon, returning to the harbour from which we would cross the lake and return to the mountain village where we lived, we went into a Catholic church. Everything was already veiled in shadows. The light shining before the Virgin, and perhaps the reserved Sacrament, has remained an unimpaired image in me.

Today, in a corner of my room in Taizé, close to the floor, an icon of the Virgin with Child is placed. Day and night, a tiny vigil light mirrors a kind of inner flame.

Since the death of Patriarch Athenagoras already long ago, that icon has taken on great significance. I can see the Patriarch of Constantinople during a visit I made to him with one of my brothers, insisting that we choose one of the icons in his cathedral for Taizé. Embarrassed by his offer (we never accept any gifts or donations, not even personal inheritances, nothing), we finally agreed to take an icon in very bad shape that had been stored on a shelf, saying that we would have it repaired when we returned home.

That dimly illuminated icon is a clear symbol. In the night of every Christian, an inner light is always fed by the mysterious presence of the Holy Spirit. It burns with a fire that never dies away.

Rejoice, full of grace!

Some of my brothers live in small fraternities among the poor and forgotten of the earth. Sometimes I spend time with them in these places where they live, in a shanty-town in Nairobi, a run-down area of New York City, in Bangladesh, or elsewhere among the poorest of the poor.

One day, when a few of my brothers and I were sharing the living conditions of a poor population living in junks on the China Sea, every afternoon we would sit down with young Asians from different countries. Together we were preparing a 'letter' to be made public upon our return.

Those young Asians wished our conversation each day to begin with the prayer of the rosary. They had been prepared for this from their childhood. Each one said the prayers in his or her own language: Chinese, Bengali, Marathi, Thai, Indonesia, Filipino, and in different European languages.

Our praying always remains simple and

words are scarcely able to describe it. It is a relief to discover in the New Testament that the apostle Paul himself wrote that he did not know how to pray as he ought. Saint Paul was no different from us, then. But he added: 'The Holy Spirit comes to help us in our weakness and intercedes for us' (Rom 8.26). So let us stop tormenting ourselves; God understands us.

Prayer never changes in its essence through the centuries, but it adopts different forms in the course of history, or at different periods in our own lives.

Some pray with no words. All is wrapped in a great silence.

Others use many words to express themselves. In the sixteenth century Teresa of Avila, a woman of great courage and realism, wrote: 'When I speak to the Lord, often I do not know what I am saying. It is love that speaks. And the soul is so beside itself that I can see no difference between it and God. Love forgets itself and says foolish things.'

Others find in the beautiful liturgy of a common worship the joy of heaven on earth, a fulfilment . . .

There are some who repeat over and over again a few words they have learned to stammer; in that way their whole being is brought into unity. How can we forget that a prayer of one's own, the same words repeated again and again, has been the incomparable support for an inner life? From the dawn of time, that has perhaps been one of the summits of prayer. Christians in the East have found it in the ceaseless praying of the Name of Jesus, while elsewhere it is the prayer, 'Rejoice, Mary, full of grace'. Such a prayer may seem to lack spontaneity, yet after long waiting, life comes surging up within.

Many are the ways of prayer that the Holy Spirit inspires in each person. Some follow one, others pursue them all. There are moments of bright certainty: Christ is there, speaking within us. But at other times he is Silence, a distant Stranger . . . No one is privileged in prayer.

Whether serene contemplation or inner struggle, prayer enables us to place everything in other hands, with the simplicity of a child, with the trust of Mary. In it a person finds energy for other struggles, for supporting a family or for transforming social conditions and making the earth a place fit to live in . . .

In a technological civilization, there is a clear break between prayer and work. When struggle and contemplation seem to be in competition, as if we had to choose one to the detriment of the other, this opposition can tear apart the very foundations of the soul.

Prayer is a serene force at work in human beings, stirring, harrowing them, never allowing them to close their eyes to evil, to wars, to all that threatens the weak of this world.

All who follow in the steps of Christ live both for other people and for God. They do not separate prayer and action.

A mother's intuition

When I arrived in Taizé in 1940, I was welcomed from the very first days by some of the old women of the village with hearts of gold. One of them, Marie Auboeuf, was for me like a mother according to the Gospel.

In those days I was alone. The community did not exist yet. I was preparing its creation and I was offering shelter to people who had to be hidden to avoid the worst. It was wartime in Europe. Marie Auboeuf was poor; she had raised ten children. Where in her heart did she find the simple intuition that allowed her to understand the vocation I was trying to live out?

That elderly woman told me that one night, many years before I arrived, while she was praying the rosary, the Virgin Mary appeared to her in a vision. The next morning, when she got up, she was cured of a paralysis of the hip that was making it harder and harder for her to walk and to take care of her children.

That appearance of the Virgin took place in Taizé long before I myself had even heard of the name of that village, and yet it still continues to have an effect.

The trust of humble men and women

When I learned one day of the death of a Portuguese immigrant who lived in our region, I went to visit his family. He was a stonemason. He had taken part in the restoration of the little Romanesque church in Taizé. He left eight children behind, some of whom were very little. The eldest son spoke of his father's last days. Following a sudden loss of blood, he asked to see a priest to receive the anointing of the sick and holy communion. The last three days, he comforted his family, assuring them that they would all meet again with Christ. Sometimes he wept, but never when his wife was present. In front of him he had an image of the Virgin. He used to kiss the image often and say: 'The Virgin is here'. With the trust of humble men and women, his last words were for her.

When she sang the 'Magnificat' the Virgin Mary, still a young girl, was able to glimpse in a prophetic vision that, as a result of the birth of her Son, the lowly would not be humiliated, but would take their full and rightful place in the human family.

I returned to that intuition when, on four different occasions, I was invited to speak about the Virgin Mary in Poland, during the Marian pilgrimage of the mine-workers of Silesia to Piekary, in the diocese of Katowice. Once I told them: 'Perhaps not one of you, Polish workers, thinks that he has an influence upon the development of the human race. But the contrary is true. It is not those who appear to be in the front ranks who bring about change in the world. Look at the Virgin Mary. Neither did she think that her life was essential for the future of the human family. Like the Mother of God, you are the humble ones of this world who are preparing the ways that lead to a future for many. Yes, your faithful waiting upon God is carrying forward many others across the earth.'

Why has God chosen us, fragile vessels of clay, to transmit a part of the mystery of Christ?

'We carry the Risen Christ in vessels of

clay,' wrote a witness to Christ nearly two thousand years ago, 'to make it clear that the radiance comes from God and not from us.' If we had only our own weak faith or our personal qualities to count upon, where would God's radiance be?

For those who agree to transmit the mystery of Christ in spite of their human frailties, for those who trust in him even in the deserts of their lives, no failures are ever final.

When days come when we find ourselves with Mary at the foot of the cross, our heart and our mind are made more universal, better able to share the pain and the distress of our fellow human beings without fear of suffering. Very often it is in the depths of the abyss that we discover the perfection of joy in communion with Jesus Christ and that, like Mary, we are given serenity of heart, a reconciled heart.

3

THE MOTHER OF JESUS

Mother Teresa

Mother of the whole world

Mary, the mother of Jesus, is also our mother. She is the mother of the whole world. When the angel announced to her the news—the Good News—that she would become the mother of Christ, she accepted as the handmaid of the Lord. At that very moment she accepted to be our mother too and that of all humanity.

Mary, our mother, is the hope of humankind. She gave us Jesus. In becoming his mother with joy, she bore the salvation and the reconciliation of the human race.

God loved the world so much that he gave his Son Jesus, entrusting him to the Virgin Mary. To prove his Father's love for the world, Jesus became so small, so helpless, that he had to have a mother to look after him.

And at the foot of the cross, too, Mary became our mother. Just before he died, Jesus gave his mother to Saint John and Saint John to his mother. And so, all of us became her children.

35

Listening to Mary

If Jesus was able to listen to his mother, the Virgin Mary, we too should be able to listen to her.

At the foot of the cross she is there, participating in the passion of Christ. She is there, constantly bringing into our life and into the life of the world joy, peace and reconciliation. She leads us to God.

In God's hands I am nothing but a tiny instrument. The Lord Jesus and Mary gave full glory to God the Father. Like them, humbly, very humbly, I wish to give full glory to God the Father.

Passing on the grace of God

Our Lady was, is, and will always remain the Mother of Jesus. One day Jesus said, 'Who is my mother? My mother is the person who does my will, who does the things that are pleasing to the Father.'

By doing the will of God, by being all for God, by saying to him, 'Be it unto me according to thy word', Mary was filled with grace. When the angel came to her and told her she was to be the mother of Jesus, she very simply said, 'Behold the handmaid of the Lord'.

When Jesus came into her life in this way, immediately Our Lady went in haste to Elizabeth to do a handmaid's work, a servant's work. And when she came to Elizabeth's house something strange happened. No one knew that in her womb Jesus was present, the Son of God. But the little unborn child in the womb of Elizabeth leapt with joy at this first contact with Christ, at the presence of God himself.

How strange that the innocent helpless

little one in the womb of his mother was chosen to be the first to recognize the coming of Christ. Like John, every single child has been created for greater things: to love and to be loved. In a way Mary was for John the most wonderful wire: she allowed God to fill her to the brim, she became full of grace which she went to pass on to John.

By surrendering ourselves to God, by saying with Our Lady 'Be it unto me according to thy word', let us ask God to use us now to go around the world, especially in our own communities, as wires connecting the hearts of men and women to the grace of God that fills us.

The closest one to priests

Mary is the closest one to priests. No one could have been a better priest than Our Lady. She really can, without difficulty, say 'This is my Body', because it was really her body that she gave to Jesus.

And yet Mary remained only the handmaid of the Lord, so that you and I can always turn to her as our Mother. She is one of our own so that we can always be one with her.

That of course is why Mary was left behind after the Ascension: to strengthen the priesthood of the apostles, to be a mother to them, until the Church, the young Church, was formed.

She was there. Just as she helped Jesus to grow, she also helped the Church to grow in the beginning. She was left behind for so many years after Jesus ascended to heaven, to help form the Church.

Still today, Our Lady has a special protection for every priest. I can imagine she must have had, and still has, a very tender love for every priest.

Houses of Nazareth

Thoughtfulness is the beginning of great sanctity.

If you learn this art of being thoughtful, you will become more and more Christ-like, for his heart was meek and he always thought of the needs of others. Our lives, to be beautiful, must be full of thought for others.

Jesus went about doing good. Our Lady did nothing else in Cana but thought of the needs of the others and made their needs known to Jesus.

The thoughtfulness of Jesus, Mary and Joseph was so great that it made the house of Nazareth the abode of God most high. If we also have that kind of thoughtfulness for each other, our homes would really become the abode of God most high, houses of Nazareth.

The quickest and the surest way to express thoughtfulness is with your tongue. If you think well of others, you will also speak well of others and to others.

From the abundance of the heart the mouth speaks. If your heart is full of love, you will speak of love and create reconciliation.

Where does this thoughtful love begin? At home. That is why it is necessary to pray together when possible. The family that prays together stays together, and if they stay together, they will love one another as God loves them.

In the silence of our hearts

Mary can teach us silence—how to keep all things in our hearts as she did, to pray in the silence of our hearts.

And then we realize that to God we are precious. He loves us and wants us to love him in return. This is especially true for us sisters who have given our word to God that we are going to belong to him.

Our vocation is but one: to belong to Jesus. To live with this conviction that nothing and nobody will separate us from the love of Christ. To love him with undivided love in chastity. Through freedom of poverty. In total surrender and obedience, and wholehearted service.

How do we put our undivided love for Christ in action? By service. By fulfilling what the Church has entrusted to us.

For us, we take a fourth vow of giving wholehearted and free service to the poorest of the poor. By this vow we depend completely on Divine Providence. We accept no Government grants, no church maintenance, no salaries, no fees, no money; we have absolutely no income. But never once have we had to say 'we don't have'. It is always there. And this is something, the word of God that he has promised, that we are more important to him than the flowers and the birds and the grass.

The ability to do our work comes from prayer. The work we do is the fruit of our union with Christ. We have been called like Mary to give Jesus to the people in the world, that through us people can look up and see his love, his compassion, his humility in action.

Our young people want holiness; they want that complete surrender to God. They will hesitate if they expect that total surrender to God and then don't find it in us.

The important thing is for all of us to come together before the Eucharist and to pray to Jesus. I think that adoration before the Eucharist is essential for our communities, whatever our age. The young sisters help us tremendously by their beautiful example of that tender love for Jesus. And the older we get, the more hungry we get for Jesus.

In our constitution we have a beautiful expression about chastity. It says there that Jesus offers his lifelong faithful personal friendship, embracing us in tenderness and love. That is a wonderful thing: God himself loves me tenderly. That is why we can have the courage and the joy and the conviction that nothing can separate us from the love of Christ.

Yes, we are precious to God. I repeat this again and again: God loves us.

Prayer

Mary, mother of Jesus, be a mother to each one of us, that we, like you, may be pure in heart; that we, like you, may love Jesus; that we, like you, may serve the poorest, for we are all poor.

4

IN MARY, A CATHOLICITY OF HEART

Brother Roger

Source of reconciliation

Week after week, as we welcome young Europeans, and young men and women from other continents, who come to Taizé to pray and to seek the wellsprings of faith, we are more and more eager to see each of them discover Christ, not in isolation, but the 'Christ of communion', Christ present in fullness in the mystery of communion which is the Church.

At the heart of this mystery, so many of the young can take the risks of an unprotected life, a life for others, of committing their whole lives and thereby becoming creators of trust and reconciliation, not only among themselves, but with people of all ages, from the very old to little children. Today, as in the first century, they have the possibility of persevering 'with one heart in prayer . . . with Mary the mother of Jesus' (Acts 1.14).

The Virgin Mary sheds light upon the roads we walk. Since the first Pentecost day, the figure of Mary has been a transparent image of the Church. With the apostles, she was able to understand that in Christ 'God's grace has appeared, the source of salvation for the whole human race' (Titus 2.11). In her, a catholicity of heart.

In Mary we can glimpse two realities essential for the Church and closely linked to one another—motherhood and catholicity. If one of these realities disappears, the other also begins to fade away. This is true for individuals as well: if a person has no experience of kindness and overflowing generosity, then they cannot hope for a generous motherhood from the Church. They remain locked up in themselves and they are in danger of remaining deaf to the Gospel's call to catholicity: 'May all be one, so that the world can believe' (John 17.21).

In the course of many centuries, from the beginnings of the Church, from the time of Mary and the apostles, the motherhood of the Church was one. Can this fundamental motherhood vanish when, at a given moment, divisions occur? Does not Mary, through her motherhood, keep the road of conversion, of a change of heart open? The more the Church is in the image of Mary, the more it is like a mother; then, the more it is possible to undergo in God a new birth, a reconciliation. In this way Mary is a source of reconciliation.

Every age has its own particular trials. Today, there is a growing number of baptized Christians who remain indifferent, not so much to Christ, but to the mystery of communion which is his Body, his Church. Often these Christians come together in groups where sometimes even esoteric practices prevail: as long as one feels comfortable together with others, nothing else matters. But when they find a way out of this kind of situation and come to understand that Christ cannot be divided, these Christians need to discover Christ as a mystery of communion. Praying with Jesus, the Risen Lord, is the way to enter more deeply into the mystery of communion of his Body, his Church. There, they can await this miracle: oneness with Jesus Christ.

These baptized Christians can be confident that they are advancing in the communion of the Church when they make the following attitude their own: preparing themselves within, day after day, to pray with Jesus and to trust in the 'Mystery of Faith' (not, of course, just the parts they would choose, but the entire 'Mystery of Faith', with no levelling of values).

To go forward on this road of trust, no one is abandoned to isolation. From the time of his resurrection, by his Holy Spirit, the mysterious presence of Christ Jesus has taken concrete shape in a communion both mystical and visible. In this mystery of communion called the Church, Christ is our visible companion by means of the believers of every age.

Trust in the Mystery of Faith

To those who aspire to follow the Christ of communion and to say to him the yes of a catholicity of heart, I would like to suggest the following prayer:

O God, I praise you for the multitudes of women, men, young people and children across the earth who seek to bear witness to trust and reconciliation. In the steps of Christ's holy witnesses of every age, from Mary and the apostles up to the present day, enable me to pray with Jesus and to prepare myself within, day after day, to trust in the 'Mystery of Faith'.

A mother's welcome

One day, another brother and I were arranging a room. In it we found a tiny icon of the Virgin and Child. It was an Eastern icon. We cleaned and polished it. Marie-Sonaly was with us; she was five and a half years old.

That icon held great meaning for us. It was a kind of symbol of a home filled with people and the warmth of a mother's welcome. In our house, those of our mothers who have already gone to be with God continue to welcome us with Mary.

Marie-Sonaly was delighted to hear these words. She was well aware that her mother is with Jesus, and she knew that Mary is with Jesus. Shortly after her birth in Calcutta, this girl had been entrusted to me and I brought her home with me. I am her godfather and every day she comes to visit me.

Children: such a joy and such a mystery in our lives! Who can tell enough all that they can communicate, through gifts unknown to them and already placed in them by the Holy Spirit? They help us to understand something of the living God by the trust they place in us, by a few words or a question they address to us, so unexpected that they awaken us to a life in God.

A yes that lasts a lifetime

In the angel's greeting to Mary, a call to
fullness, to a catholicity of heart, rings out:
'Rejoice, you who are full of grace'. This
call is universal; it is true for every Christian: 'Rejoice, my soul, full of grace', 'Rejoice, Church, full of grace'. Trust in God
makes it possible for everyone to choose
the way which leads upward to serene joy.

To make Mary's answer to the angel a
reality in our lives, it is good to remember
that for centuries before the coming of
Christ there had existed within the people
of Israel a community of humble believers.
The Virgin Mary belonged to that community. These poor men and women of
God were eagerly looking forward to a
fulfilment as they continued in faith to
await the Messiah. Waiting, trusting in
God in this way, renders a person ready
and open to whatever comes. By responding to the angel's announcement with a yes,
by her inward consent, Mary committed
herself to a lifelong fidelity. In this way,

throughout history, God has safeguarded the holiness of the call already addressed to Abraham and to his people in former times.

A commitment for life brings us face to face with the unknown. This yes can awaken in us a question: how can we remain faithful when no human being is built naturally for a total gift of self? Let the day of peaceful consent come, when wonder suffuses our life like dew. Then we see clearly that the Holy Spirit has placed a yes in the depths of our being; and when we commit ourselves by saying yes to God, even an element of human error is gradually transfigured.

Praying with Mary means praying the same words that rose from her heart of hearts in response to the angel: 'May it be done unto me according to your will'. To accomplish his will, God asks us neither to destroy nor to exalt human desire but, in inner silence, to gather it up into an even greater desire: the passion for the 'Christ of communion', his Church. In it, day by day Christ becomes our essential love, a poem of love with God.

In this respect, today the expectations of many of the young are both enthusiastic and characterized by seriousness. Their authentic longings, far from leading them to follow the fashions of the day, enable them to discover the realities of the Kingdom made accessible and even visible. And a way opens for them on which the taste for the gift of life becomes one with the taste for the gift of the Kingdom. When their elders walk on this same road, the hopes of the young are stimulated. There is nothing to fear. The Church brings these gifts to life and rediscovers them again and again; they are never taken away from her. In the presence of such gifts, already offered in Christ before the world began, the day of the fullness of a trust dawns at last.

If there is a sentence in the Gospel that is a reflection of Mary, it is certainly the sixth Beatitude: happy the pure in heart; they shall see God (Matt. 5.8). They will see him like Mary who attentively 'pondered all these things in her heart' and saw God with her inward eye.

My brothers and I, responding to a calling that is monastic in essence and committed by a yes to celibacy for life, are penetrated with the significance of the sixth Beatitude. In the transparency of our being, body, mind and soul, God allows himself to be discovered as our essential love. In that way a unity between personal identity and faith is slowly forged and takes shape.

And in the yes of married life, limpidity of heart, a transparent heart, turns our eyes towards the living God.

Mary's yes can sustain the faithfulness of an entire lifetime. On account of Christ and the Gospel, a yes for life is a fire. Such a yes makes us vulnerable. It cannot be otherwise. But this yes keeps us awake. Little by little, it builds us up within and enables us to move ahead towards life everlasting.

Prayer

Lord Christ, for anyone who understands your call to say a yes for life, hesitation and fear can spring up.

But we know that by your Holy Spirit you have placed this yes in the depths of our being, down to the regions of the unconscious—the yes which was in Mary. And one day we are astonished to find ourselves already on the road, following in your footsteps.

This yes keeps us alert. How could we fall asleep when the Church is shaken on all sides and when the world is ridden with trials.

This yes leaves us vulnerable. But you offer it for ever and it is in everyone.

Giving what God gives us

At a time when he was preparing to commit himself for life in our community of Taizé, one of my brothers, Hector, received a letter from his mother that he wanted to show to me.

His mother lives in New York City. She is Peurto Rican. Almost every day one of the poor people of the neighbourhood calls upon her to come to the bedside of someone dying; there she prays the rosary. This woman had only one son; Hector is an only child. Knowing that her son was committing himself for life in our community, she wrote him the following lines to let him know that she consented to his vocation:

'As I was reading in your letter of your total love for God, I saw the Virgin Mary pass before my eyes. As a woman and a mother, she too suffered for her son, knowing that the one she bore would be crucified later for his people. Accepting what God has already disposed gradually purifies the heart. My son, what can I, as your mother, refuse you? What can I, as your mother, demand of you? What can I do when it is God who is acting and disposing? I cannot refuse God what belongs to him. I give him the little I have. You are my life, you are all that I have but, seeing the love God has for us, we have to give him everything.'

This mother gave what God gave her. Not everyone, of course, feels able to give such a gift right away. They need a lot of time for a peaceful inner consent to spring up little by little in them.

By her life, Mary accomplished the gesture of offering. She did not hold back for herself what God gave her; she offered her Son to the world. In her a source of reconciliation becomes visible. From that source can be drawn the audacity to live the Gospel's call to forgiveness, to reconciliation, in short to giving what God gives us.

MOTHER TERESA OF CALCUTTA

BROTHER ROGER OF TAIZE

Mother Teresa of Calcutta

Mother Teresa, or Agnes Ganxhe Bojaxhiu as she was then known, was·born on the 27th August, 1910, in Skopje, Yugoslavia, of Albanian parents. Already at the age of twelve she felt that she had a vocation to the religious life and six years later, caught up in the wave of enthusiasm for the missions evoked by the writings of Pope Pius XI and inspired by letters written by a Yugoslav jesuit about his work in Kurson, Agnes became convinced that her calling was to become a missionary. Accordingly she sought admission into the Congregation of Loreto nuns who worked in Bengal and, after an initial period spent learning English at the Loreto Abbey in Rathfarnham, Dublin, was sent to India to begin her novitiate in Darjeeling, a hill station in the Himalayas. Following her first vows she became a teacher at a high school of girls run by the Loreto Sisters in Calcutta and for more than fifteen years taught, among other subjects, history and geography to successive generations of Bengali girls, eventually becoming the school's headmistress. Increasingly, however, she became aware of the desperate and unattended needs of those who occupied the slums beyond the convent walls; and increasingly she realized that her role was not within the structure of organised education but among the very poorest of the poor, the least of Christ's brethren. On the 10th September 1946, in a rattling, congested train, taking her to a retreat in Darjeeling, she heard what she describes as a 'call within a call'. She had already been called to the religious life, and to her there was never any question of abandoning it; but now she was being called to another form of service within that life. The message was quite clear! 'I was to leave the convent and help the poor whilst living among them. It was an order. To fail it would have been to break the faith.'

So it was that in 1948, dressed in a simple cotton sari, Mother Teresa left behind her the relative security of the Loreto school in Calcutta and stepped out into the city's streets to live as one with the poorest of the poor and to found a new Congregation committed to their service. She began by opening a small school in the slums. The school was an open space among the hovels, the children squatted in the dirt and Mother Teresa scratched the letters of the Bengali alphabet in the mud with a stick. In 1954 the plight of those reduced to dying in the streets because overcrowded hospitals refused to accept the obviously incurable induced her to open the first 'home for the dying' where Hindus, Muslims and Christians alike could die with dignity, having received the rituals of their own particular faith. The work grew. Mother Teresa's Missionaries of Charity cared for an increasing number of orphaned, sick, crippled or mentally handicapped children. They provided treatment, training and above all love for lepers and indeed for all those with whom Christ in St Matthew's gospel had specifically identified himself. (Matt. 25.40).

Mother Teresa dedicated her congregation to the Immaculate Heart of Mary in the conviction that it was born through the intercession of the Virgin. She encouraged the Sisters to strive to be like Mary because Mary of all created beings presents the most perfect likeness of God, and like the Mother of God they must seek in all humility, to empty themselves of 'self' in order that Christ might be present in them. In addition to the usual vows of poverty, chastity and obedience the Missionaries of Charity make a fourth commitment 'to offer wholehearted free service to the poorest of the poor'. The 'poorest of the poor' in whom they identify the suffering Christ crying out for love are the hungry, the thirsty, the naked, the homeless, the dying destitutes, the captive, the crippled, the leprosy sufferers; they are also the alcoholics, the drug addicts, the bereaved, the unloved, those who are a burden to human society, who have lost all faith in life. Experience of life in more efficent countries has brought Mother Teresa and those who work with her to the realisation that the spiritual poverty the loneliness, the lack of love in the West is a more acute problem and one which is more difficult to solve than the material poverty of the so called 'Third World'. Thus today the mission which began so unpretentiously in some of India's most disease-ridden slums is a universal one. There are now scattered throughout the world some 3,000 Sisters and 600 Brothers, and an association of three million Co-Workers or lay-helpers of a wide variety of nationalities, faiths and denominations who share the commitment and the spirituality of the Missionaries of Charity. This 'success', Mother Teresa insists is not hers, she is only 'the little pencil in God's hand', and the secret of such growth is 'faith in the joyous insecurity of Divine Providence,' prayer—the solution to every insoluble problem, and the constant awareness that she is but a channel for God's particular love for the suffering poor of this world.

68

Brother Roger of Taizé

Brother Roger, the founder of the Taizé Community, has devoted his life to searching for ways to overcome the divisions between Christians and those in the human family. Taizé has become a place where hundreds of thousands of young adults from Europe and from other continents go to pray and to prepare themselves to promote peace and reconciliation throughout the world.

In 1940 the Second World War was raging. Brother Roger was 25 years old, and carried within himself the dream of creating a monastic community devoted to reconciliation. He decided to leave Switzerland, his father's native country, since he felt things were too tranquil there, and settle in France, where his mother's family originated. He wanted to live among people who were suffering from the consequences of war.

When he is asked what contributed to his early decisions, Brother Roger often replies by recalling his mother's mother. During the First World War, she was a widow living in the North of France. Her three sons were fighting on the front lines. Despite the bombing, she insisted on staying in her home to offer shelter to refugees—old people, children, pregnant women. She only left at the very last moment, when everyone had to flee. Brother Roger's grandmother was deeply concerned that no one should ever again have to experience what she had experienced. Separated Christians were killing one another in Europe: if they at least could be reconciled, perhaps another war could be avoided. She was from an old Protestant family. To accomplish without delay a reconciliation within herself, she went to a Catholic church. Brother Roger writes: 'It was as if she realized that, in the Catholic Church, the Eucharist was a source of unanimity of the faith.' And he continued: 'In reconciling within herself the current of faith of her Protestant origins with the faith of the Catholic Church, she was able to live in such a way that she did not appear to be repudiating her own people.'

These two realities which his grandmother lived out—taking care of the poor and becoming reconciled with the faith of the Catholic Church—would mark Brother Roger's entire life. At the beginning of the Second World War, he decided to settle alone in the village of Taizé, less than two miles from the line of demarcation that divided France in half. There he bought a house and hid political refugees,

69

especially Jews, who were fleeing the last occupation. 'The more a human being wants to live something absolute for God,' he would later write, 'the more essential it is to live out this absolute in a situation of human distress.'

Brother Roger remained in Taizé from 1940 to 1942. At that time he was already praying morning, noon and evening in a tiny chapel. But since the Gestapo, the Nazi police, visited the house on several occasions, he had to leave France from late 1942 to the end of 1944. When he returned, he was accompanied by his first three brothers whom he had met in the meantime.

Over the years, more young men have come to join the community. The brothers take monastic commitments, committing themselves for life to celibacy and to life together. Today the Taizé Community includes over eighty brothers, Catholics or of Protestant origin, from some twenty different countries. By its very existence it is thus a sign of reconciliation both between divided Christians and between different nations. It forms what Brother Roger calls a 'parable of communion'.

As soon as the community numbered twelve brothers, in the 1950s, Brother Roger asked some of them to go and live at key points in the world, to be alongside those who were suffering. In small groups, in Asia, Africa, North and South America, they share the living conditions of poor districts. Brother Roger himself goes to stay in places of suffering. Among other areas, he has spent time in Chile after the coup d'état there, in a slum in Calcutta, in South Africa, Lebanon, Haiti, and in the region of sub-Saharan Africa suffering from drought. Each year he travels to Eastern European countries as well.

Since 1966, sisters of Saint Andrew, a Catholic community founded 750 years ago, have been living in the neighbouring village of Amougny. They collaborate with the brothers in the work of welcoming the many visitors to Taizé.

The community accepts no gifts or donations and has no capital in reserve. The brothers do not even accept any personal inheritances. They work for their living.

Brother Roger was invited to attend the Second Vatican Council and has had regular meetings with Popes John XXIII, Paul VI and, currently, John Paul II. In 1986, Pope John Paul II came to Taizé and aid to the brothers: 'I would like to express to you my affection and my trust with these simple words, with which Pope John XXIII, who loved you so much, greeted Brother Roger one day: "Ah, Taizé, that little springtime!" '

Since 1957-1958, Taizé has welcomed young people in ever increasing numbers. From Portugal to Finland, from Ireland to Yugoslavia, as well as from Africa, Asia, Australia, South and North America, they take part in week-long international meetings centred on a deepening of the wellsprings of faith. Hundreds of thousands of young adults have thus received not only an experience of prayer and a universal vision of the Church, but also an international awareness, a sense of trust in people from other countries and a concern for human rights.

In Lebanon, at Christmas 1982, Brother Roger proposed the beginning of a 'pilgrimage of trust on earth'. Prayer celebrations mark topping-points on this pilgrimage. They are always prepared months in advance together with local parishes and congregations, and they bring together thousands in the cities of Northern and Eastern Europe: Paris, London, Rome, Barcelona, Cologne, Dresden, Dublin, Madrid, East Berlin, Warsaw, and so on. In 1985 the Taizé Community organized an intercontinental meeting of young adults in Madras, India, attended by young people from some forty-five different countries.

Young people from every continent are thus associated in a common search for the roots of their faith. Taizé has never wanted to create a 'movement' with them, however, preferring instead to encourage them to commit themselves in the places where they live—in their neighbourhoods, their parishes, their towns and villages.

Concerned that every human life be respected, Brother Roger sometimes makes public gestures for peace. In doing this he is often accompanied by children of several different continents to indicate that this gesture is undertaken on behalf of those whose future is threatened. He went to meet the American and Soviet ambassadors in Madrid in 1983, and the Secretary General of the United Nations in 1985.

This concern for peace and reconciliation is present in all of Brother Roger's books, which have been translated into ten languages. In 1952, he wrote what later became 'the sources of Taizé', to indicate for his

71

brothers the essential of their vocation. Every two or three years he publishes a book whose title is in itself a challenge: *Living Today for God, Festival without End, Struggle and Contemplation, A Life We Never Dared Hope For, The Wonder of a Love, And Your Deserts Shall Flower, A Heart that Trusts.*

DATE DUE